CLASSIC BALLPARKS

JAMES BUCKLEY JR.

BARNES
& NOBLE
BOOKS

NEW YORK

This edition published by Barnes & Noble, Inc.,
by arrangement with becker&mayer!

2004 Barnes & Noble Books

M 10 9 8 7 6 5 4 3 2 1

ISBN 0-7607-6008-X

Produced in partnership and licensed by Major League Baseball, Inc.

Major League Baseball trademarks and copyrights are used with permission of Major League Baseball Properties, Inc. These include, but are not limited to, the following: All-Star Game®, Fall Classic®, Fenway Park™, Green Monster™, Major League Baseball®, Midsummer Classic®, Tiger Stadium™, World Series®, Wrigley Field™, and Yankee Stadium™.

For my grandfather, who took my dad to the Jury Box in Braves Field; for my father, who took me to my first Major League game at Fenway Park in 1972; and for my son, Conor, who caught a foul ball when we went to his first American League game in Anaheim in 2003 (the lucky stiff!).

Editorial: Ben Raker
Design: Todd Bates
Image research: Shayna Ian
Production coordination: Cindy Lashley
Project management: Sheila Kamuda

Library of Congress Cataloging-in-Publication data is available.

Printed in China.

CONTENTS

Author's Note

Before we begin this tour of America's most historic ballparks, a word about the dimensions noted inside. For each ballpark, a box is shown with relevant information, including the number of feet from home plate to various points of the outfield fences. These are, especially in the late and lamented parks, in many cases approximations based on the best available research. Fences moved in and out over time (in some cases depending on who the opponent was), so coming up with exact measurements is problematic. In fact, the Boston Red Sox refuse to have the distance to their left-field corner measured, preferring to make it more of a mystery than a fact just how far the Green Monster is from home plate. So take these distances (as well as the similarly fluctuating capacity figures) with a grain of salt (or a handful of ballpark peanuts).

I'd also like to note here the invaluable contributions of dozens of baseball researchers and writers whose much longer and vastly more detailed works were consulted extensively for this little tribute to green slices of heaven. Several works stand out and are recommended to the reader interested in further study. Among these are *Diamonds: The Evolution of the Ballpark* by the late (and also lamented) Michael Gershman; *Green Cathedrals* by Philip J. Lowry (a great source for ballpark-related stats); and *Lost Ballparks* by Lawrence S. Ritter. Thanks also to my colleague Jim Gigliotti for his research assistance.

Finally, a personal ballpark story that my friends (and doctors) will appreciate. In 1981, just before a game in which my beloved Red Sox were visiting the then-California Angels, I was hit by a car while running haphazardly through the Anaheim Stadium parking lot. My left forearm was badly broken and metal plates were inserted to mend the arm, and they remain there today. In 1985, while departing a game at the Oakland Coliseum (after again viewing the visiting Red Sox), I found myself amid a scuffle, the end result of which was a severe compound fracture of my *right* forearm. Swear to God. Mirror X-rays, identical scars, more plates and screws.

The point of this story is twofold: One, being a devoted fan of all baseball and ballparks, I still go to games as often as I can, even given this checkered and painful past. Two, as my mother still reminds me twenty years later, please be careful when traveling to games.

I'd like to keep my story unique.

–J.B.
Santa Barbara, California

INTRODUCTION

For America's beautiful ballparks, it is, actually, very easy being green. As one looks at the nostalgia-soaked writings about ballparks of today and long ago, that is the word that crops up over and over: green. Verdant green. Emerald green. Green fields of heaven. Green brighter than Rita Hayworth's eyes. It's the grass, of course, that has led so many poets (and wanna-be poets) to wax, well, poetically, about the sprawling, glowing outfields of dreams. So while this book is about ballparks themselves—the actual buildings in which generations of fans watched the game—what those fans took away from those trips were memories of the fields: the color of the grass and the eternal springtime it represented.

The Major League Baseball season begins, with the eternal thanks of the poets, in the spring, when that grass is just a-bloomin' in said fields. The first sites for the game were, in fact, just that—simple fields, perhaps fallow between plantings or empty save for meadowlarks and dandelions. When that magical measurement of

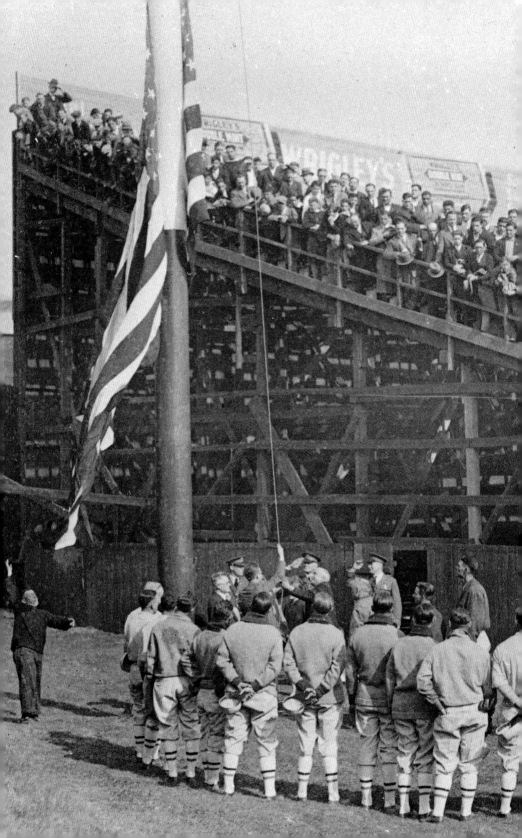

90 feet between bases was paced out and a spot for home plate established, a random, wild field became a baseball diamond.

At first, of course, there weren't even fences. Every homer was an inside-the-park job. How wonderful that the site of what is regarded as the very first baseball game played under rules recognizable today was a place in New Jersey known as the Elysian Fields. A "happy place" (*elysium* in Greek) indeed, on June 19, 1846, when the Knickerbocker Club (that had formed baseball's basic rules) lost to the New York Nine 23-1.

As would be the case throughout baseball history from just about that point on, commerce soon stepped in to rule the day. In 1858, fans were first charged admission to a game, an all-star affair played at Fashion Race Course on Long Island. (Author Michael Gershman notes that this park is perhaps "three hundred yards from [what today is the site of] Shea Stadium.") After discovering that fans were watching games for free from the unenclosed outfields, club owners looked for an answer and found it in wood. The Union Grounds opened in Brooklyn in 1862, the first enclosed ballpark in history. Though opening day, May 16, 1862, was free, admission was charged thereafter.

By the time the National Association, the first professional league, was formed in 1871, wooden ballparks were found in most cities. Typically, they had a single level of bleacher-type seating spreading from behind home plate up both foul lines. Most did not feature outfield seating; in fact, some parks reserved outfield space for patrons' horse-drawn coaches. Fans could park and watch the game in style, somewhat like a drive-in movie theater. Amenities were added to various parks over the next decades, including luxury boxes atop the bleachers, press boxes, outfield bleachers, and special ladies' benches.

The 1890s saw several disastrous ballpark fires, with the all-wood construction providing ample combustible material. In their places, sturdier ballparks were built (though wood remained a key ingredient), and owners continued their drive to create "grounds" that would bring both the high-class and the hoi polloi.

By 1903, organized baseball was referred to as the "Major Leagues" and was divided into American League and National League teams. There were a total of sixteen teams, all of whom played in the best parks in their home cities. But owners were realizing that the experience a fan enjoyed on game day would markedly impact their bottom line. There was no TV money, no radio money, very little advertising money. Attracting fans to the gate was practically a team's sole source of income, so creating a way to attract and seat more and more fans became a key goal of the expanding leagues. The years before World War I saw a boom in the building of larger ballparks, using then-modern engineering methods, most with an eye to improving comfort and attractiveness as well as to increasing capacity.

The results of that ballpark-building boom are showcased in this book, which celebrates five of the best of the ballparks of that era, beginning with the final incarnation of the Polo Grounds in 1911 and stretching to Wrigley Field in 1914. This was the age of the "jewel box" ballparks—parks that made frequent use of the then-new steel-and-concrete construction technique. Fans today still enjoy the benefits of these jewel boxes, as they sit in Fenway Park or Wrigley Field. The book wraps up with another huge step in ballpark evolution: the opening of Yankee Stadium, when the pastoral ballparks rose up to become the muscular structures more often seen today. Money (and Babe Ruth) made that expansion possible, but one wonders if a little of the romance was left behind.

> "When that magical measurement of 90 feet between bases was paced out and a spot for home plate established, a random, wild field became a baseball diamond."

Chapter One
THE POLO GROUNDS

Few sites in baseball history have seen as much, well, baseball history as the Polo Grounds, the only ballpark ever to be home to three different Major League teams. The Polo Grounds wasn't a ballfield, it was a pasture. Its center field was almost as deep as two Fenway Park fields put together. Yet its right-field corner was one of the closest to the plate in baseball history.

The longest-lived and most famous Polo Grounds was actually the fifth of five ballparks in upper Manhattan known by that name. The first was used from 1883 to 1888 and was literally what its name said: a polo field, owned by James Gordon Bennett, publisher of the *New York Herald*. But the city kicked the New York Giants out of that park (at 110th Street and Fifth Avenue) and then-owner John Day found a field farther north on the island. On this site, below Coogan's Bluff, three variations on the diamond theme rose and fell over the years from 1889 to 1911. During that time, the Giants boasted some of the most legendary names in Major League Baseball, including manager John McGraw. McGraw's ace was Hall of Famer Christy Mathewson, who made history in the 1905 World Series by pitching three shutouts in the space of six days. The third clinched the World Series at the Polo Grounds; Mathewson's 0.00 ERA and stunning record of eighteen strikeouts against only one walk remain World Series bests.

Following pages: The Polo Grounds took on its distinctive oval shape in 1911, when the fifth of five ballparks known by this name was built in upper Manhattan. It is shown here after 1922, when further renovations were made.

THE POLO GROUNDS

Ballpark Basics

Location: Upper Manhattan, west side of
Eighth Avenue between 157th and 159th Streets

Date opened: June 28, 1911

Approximate cost: $250,000

Tenants: New York Giants, 1911–1957; New York Yankees,
1913–1922; New York Mets, 1962–1963 (only park to have been
the home field of three different Major League teams)

Outfield distances: Left field: 277 feet; Left-center field: 450 feet;
Center field: 433 feet (since 1911) to 483 feet (since 1963);
Right-center field: 445 feet; Right field: 257 feet

Largest crowd: 64,471, September 13, 1936

Capacity: 56,000

Home team W-L records: New York Giants at home (1911–1957): 2,086-1,455;
New York Yankees at home (1913–1922): 416-335; New York Mets at home
(1962–1963): 56-105

Last home run: Jim Hickman, New York Mets (September 18, 1963)

Player with most home runs: Mel Ott, New York Giants (323)

Number of no-hit games pitched (and most recent): 6 (most recent: Rex Barney,
Brooklyn Dodgers vs. New York Giants, September 9, 1948)

Other events/sports: Hosted Major League Baseball All-Star Game in 1934 and 1942
. . . Site of many famous boxing matches, including heavyweight champion Jack
Dempsey's knockout of challenger Luis Firpo in 1923. More than 82,000 fans—the
largest crowd in Polo Grounds history—watched that fight . . . Home for various pro
football teams, including the NFL's New York Giants (1925–1955) and the AFL's
New York Jets (1960–1963; the club was known as the Titans for its first three
seasons) . . . The 1934 NFL Championship Game between the Giants and Chicago
Bears took place at the Polo Grounds. New York trailed 13-3 in the second half before
donning basketball shoes on an icy field and winning the "Sneakers Game" 30-13.

Unusual ground rules: The bullpens in left-center field and right-center field were
part of fair territory . . . A five-foot-high memorial to veteran Eddie Grant, a former
Major League player who was killed in World War I, was in play at the base of
the clubhouse wall in deepest center field.

The most well known and longest-lasting of the five Polo Grounds structures opened in June 1911, two months after the April fire that had destroyed much of the ballpark. Giants owner John T. Brush realized the advantage of modern building techniques and made his new park one of the first concrete-and-steel buildings in the majors. Below the famous Coogan's Bluff hillside, Brush built a double-deck ballpark with stands that extended to the outfield corners, with a single deck of bleachers across the distant outfield. The field itself had a rather odd shape, much like a bathtub or a race course. Though less than 300 feet to each outfield corner, it plunged to nearly 500 feet in dead center field. The park had one of the largest outfields ever, and also featured extensive foul territory.

The facades of the second deck featured Roman-inspired friezes, while the coats of arms of all the National League teams adorned the wall high above center field. In a unique twist, the clubhouse was located in a structure in center field, rather than underneath the ballpark behind home plate as in most other parks. Players thus had to make the long trek across the outfield to reach the showers, a walk that felt longer, of course, after losing. At the base of that center-field wall, near the bottom of the steps that players climbed to reach the clubhouse, was a five-foot concrete monument. It was erected to honor former Giants player Eddie Grant, who died during World War I, and it was in play on the field itself.

Fans could still stand on Coogan's Bluff to watch games, however, as they had since the very first games were played on the site in

> "The Polo Grounds wasn't a ballfield, it was a pasture. Its center field was almost as deep as two Fenway Park fields put together."

Following pages: Over the years, the Polo Grounds was home to three New York ballclubs: the Giants (pictured here before a game, circa 1957), the Yankees, and the Mets.

Poor Fred Merkle

The Polo Grounds pre-1911 was witness to one of the most famous foul-ups of all time. Fred Merkle was an up-and-coming outfielder with the Giants, who actually would go on to have a long and successful pro career. It got off to a horrible start, however.

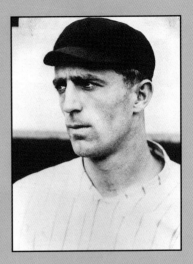

On September 23, 1908, the Cubs visit the Giants with the two teams essentially tied for first place. With the score tied at 1-1 with two outs in the bottom of the ninth, Merkle is on first when a single knocks in the winning run. Merkle heads across the outfield, thinking the game is over. The fans swarm the field. But the Cubs notice that Merkle has not touched second base. They literally battle the crowd for the ball in order to touch second and force Merkle out, negating the run. In the melee, the umpires side with the Cubs, call Merkle out, and the game is declared (and later upheld by the league) as a 1-1 tie. Merkle is vilified, and his place in infamy is assured when the season itself ends with the two teams tied.

A playoff game was held on October 8 to determine the league champion, and though the Giants had future Hall of Famer Christy Mathewson on the hill, they lost to the Cubs 4-2.

Above: New York Giants outfielder Fred Merkle, shown here after his infamous 1908 blunder.

1891. They looked down from the heights on the park that would become part of Major League lore forever in 1951 (see page 24). Inside, a then Major League high 34,000 fans watched from a closer vantage point.

What all those fans, freeloaders, and paying customers watched was, for several decades, among the best ball played anywhere. The New York Giants were consistent winners, capturing eight NL pennants from 1911 to 1924 and winning World Series in 1921 and 1922. Not only that, but the park was home to the New York Yankees for 10 seasons (1913–1922)—the 1921 World Series played between these two New York "roomies" was the only World Series in which all the games were played at the same ballpark. The time that the Yankees spent at the Polo Grounds included the

Above: The Polo Grounds, in the 1950s. **Following pages:** A day game at the Polo Grounds before 1911 when center-field bleachers were installed.

debut season (in Yankees pinstripes) of a kid named Babe Ruth. Ruth adored the short right-field fence in the Polo Grounds, which was perfectly suited to his mighty left-handed swing, and he began his rise to the top of the home run charts with 54 in 1920 and 59 in 1921. (Win a bar bet by asking how many homers Ruth hit in 1921 in Yankee Stadium. The answer, of course, is none.)

Ruth and the Yankees moved out in 1923, when their own edifice rose within sight of the Polo Grounds, across the Harlem River in the

Above: Giants outfielder Bobby Thomson, who in 1951 hit one of history's most famous home runs at the Polo Grounds. He is shown here in the early 1950s.

Magical Moments

October 14, 1905
Giants and Christy Mathewson win World Series over Athletics.

September 23, 1908
Giants outfielder Fred Merkle makes
infamous mistake (see page 18).

October 8, 1908
Giants lose to Cubs in NL playoff game.

October 13, 1921
Giants win World Series over Yankees.

October 8, 1922
Giants win World Series over Yankees.

July 10, 1934
Giants pitcher Carl Hubbell strikes out five
straight future Hall of Famers in All-Star Game.

August 1, 1945
Mel Ott's 500th home run.

October 3, 1951
Bobby Thomson's homer wins NL pennant over Dodgers.

September 29, 1954
Willie Mays makes amazing catch as Giants win first
game of four-game World Series sweep over Indians.

April 13, 1962
New York Mets play first home game in front of 12,447 fans.

Bronx (see page 113). To match his new and larger rival, Brush completed the enclosure of his grounds and increased the capacity to more than 54,000.

The Giants returned to the World Series in 1933, 1936, and 1937. They won in '33, but watched as their former parkmates rose to dominate the sport both in the city and the nation. It was the Yankees who knocked off the Giants in '36 and '37. It was left to the Yankees, too, to dim somewhat the single most famous moment in Polo Grounds history, if not the game's history.

"Willie Mays' famous catch and the heroics of pinch-hitter Dusty Rhodes helped the Giants win their last championship of the century, and their last ever in New York."

The 1951 season ended with the Giants and Brooklyn Dodgers tied for first place in the National League. A three-game playoff was called for to decide the pennant, and the teams split the first two games. The third game was played at the Polo Grounds on October 3.

The Dodgers led an exciting game by a seemingly comfortable 4-1 margin going into the bottom of the ninth inning. New York's Whitey Lockman doubled in a run to cut the Brooklyn lead to two runs and leave two men on base. Outfielder Bobby Thomson was up and reliever Ralph Branca (foreshadowing time: Branca's uniform number was 13) was called into the game. While favorite trivia answer Willie Mays waited on deck, Thomson lined Branca's second pitch into the short porch in left field for a stunning, historic, game-winning, pennant-winning three-run homer. Giants radio announcer Russ Hodges' frantic call of the action would become as famous as Thomson's "Shot Heard 'Round the World." "The Giants win the pennant!

Right: Hall of Fame outfielder Willie Mays, in a 1950s New York Giants uniform.

The Catch

It was not exactly a home-field advantage, but the immense center-field expanse at the Polo Grounds was partly responsible for the single most famous defensive play in Major League Baseball history. As any fan worth his or her peanuts knows, Willie Mays made "The Catch" in the deep well of the Polo Grounds center field in Game 1 of the 1954 World Series.

Chasing down a long drive by Cleveland's Vic Wertz, Mays caught the ball over his shoulder on a dead run, more than 470 feet from home plate. Catching and then whirling and throwing in one motion, Mays' play kept the Giants from losing Game 1 of a World Series they would eventually sweep over the heavily-favored Indians. The fact that it came in the World Series, was performed by one of baseball's all-time greats, and happened in the depths of the Polo Grounds outfield—plus the great early TV shots of the event—have cemented "The Catch" as a monument not only to glovework, but to the differences between the huge parks of yesteryear and the homer-inducing parks of today.

The Giants win the pennant! The Giants win the pennant!" screamed Hodges.

After this dramatic moment, the Giants would lose in the World Series to the Yankees. Nevertheless, Thomson's amazing homer was enshrined forever near the top of the game's magical moments as the "Miracle of Coogan's Bluff."

Three years later, in 1954, the Giants did bring a world championship back to Coogan's Bluff by defeating the mighty Cleveland Indians. Willie Mays' famous catch (see box) and the heroics of pinch-hitter Dusty Rhodes (two homers, seven RBI, .667 average) helped the Giants win their last championship of the century, and their last ever in New York.

The reason for such finality is that, with the soon-to-be Los Angeles Dodgers needing a traveling partner on the West Coast, and with San Francisco beckoning with open arms, the Giants left New York and the Polo Grounds after the 1957 season. Their final game there was a 9-1 loss to the Pirates on September 29, 1957, before only 11,606 fans. There was some outrage at the time of the move, but with the Yankees just a Mickey Mantle homer across the Harlem River, few if any fans mourned the passing of the Giants as much as the romantic Brooklynites bemoaned the loss of their Dodgers (see page 85). In Manhattan, it seemed, the now–San Francisco Giants were barely missed.

"What all those fans, freeloaders, and paying customers watched was, for several decades, among the best ball played anywhere."

The Polo Grounds itself, however, unlike the beloved Ebbets Field in Brooklyn (chapter four), did enjoy a brief renaissance. In 1962, the National League awarded an expansion franchise to New York, and the New York Mets were born. The Mets needed a place to play while a new stadium was built for them in Queens (Shea Stadium), and the still-standing Polo Grounds served quite well. Casey Stengel, who had helped the Giants win two World Series as a speedy outfielder and then skippered the Yankees to seven World Series titles, was picked to lead what would become the standard for bad baseball teams. The 1962 Mets lost an all-time record 120 games. They kept it up in 1963, losing 111 more, the last one of which was the final game ever played at the Polo Grounds, a 5-1 loss to Philadelphia.

In 1964 the Polo Grounds came crashing down, razed by the same wrecking ball that had destroyed Ebbets Field two years earlier. The park is now a housing project, but the memories created by McGraw, Mathewson, Merkle, Mays, and many others live on.

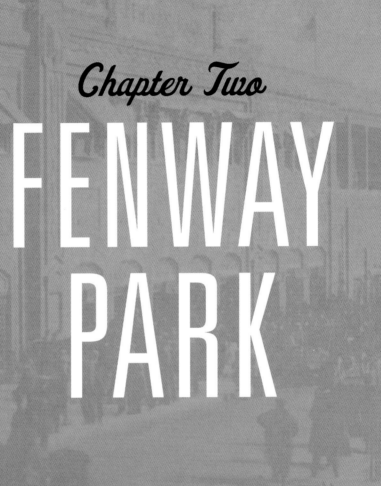

Chapter Two

FENWAY PARK

I f you're ever in Boston, here's a quick translation for something you might hear on the street. When a ruddy-faced Boston Irishman mumbles something about "Fenwhay Pahk in Kenmoah Squayah," he is speaking of heaven.

If there is one ballpark in this book that America, Major League Baseball, and the world can't do without, it's Fenway Park. Fenway Park is the quintessential old-time ballpark. Lovingly called "that little jewel box of a park" by John Updike, it is more than just a place to watch a ballgame. It's a place to relive history, to play a personal part in a 150-year love affair with a game, to experience what the game was for our grandfathers, our fathers, and players whose names are just legends to today's fans.

All this lovin' started on April 20, 1912. The project had been started the previous September by Red Sox owner John Taylor, but Taylor was less interested in baseball and more interested in the ball-park as the centerpiece of a real estate empire in a then-little-used backwater of Beantown. He sold the team in December, and the new owners, Jimmy McAleer and Robert McRoy, kept the ballpark project moving. The main part of the seating sections consisted of steel-and-concrete risers with oak seating. The outfield bleachers and the stands along the foul lines were all wood.

Opening day saw—ironically, given later events—a victory over the New York AL team, then known as the Highlanders but later to

Following pages: Fenway Park in its opening year, 1912.

FENWAY PARK

Ballpark Basics

Location: Boston, Kenmore Square

Date opened: April 20, 1912

Approximate cost: $650,000

Tenants: Boston Red Sox, 1912–present; Boston Braves (1913–1915)

Outfield distances: Left field: 310 feet; Left-center field: 379 feet; Center field: 420 feet (since 1963); Right-center field: 380 feet; Right field: 302 feet.

Largest crowd: 47,627, September 22, 1935

Capacity (2003): 33,781

Home team W-L records: Boston Red Sox at home (1912–present): 4,025-3,052 (through 2003); Boston Braves at home (1913–1915): 53-27

First home run: Hugh Bradley, Boston Red Sox (April 26, 1912)

Last home run: not applicable

Player with most home runs: Ted Williams, Boston Red Sox (248)

Number of no-hit games pitched (and most recent): 12 (Derek Lowe, Boston Red Sox vs. Tampa Bay, April 27, 2002)

Other events/sports: Hosted Major League Baseball All-Star Game in 1946, 1961, and 1999 . . . Used as a major rock-concert venue for the first time in September 2003 by Bruce Springsteen . . . Home of the National Football League's Boston Redskins (1933–1936) and Boston Yanks (1944–1948), and the American Football League's Boston Patriots (1963–1968).

Unusual ground rules: Any ball that hits a ladder on the Green Monster is in play (the ladder begins more than 13 feet above the ground and extends to the top of the wall) . . . Until 1970, a flagpole stood several feet in front of the wall on the warning track in left-center field. The pole was in play.

be called the Yankees, a team that would cause so much grief and angst all over New England. The park was an immediate hit with fans and players alike. Along the base of the left-field barrier that would someday become known simply as The Wall was a slope of dirt that rose 10 feet up the structure. When not covered with fans, the slope became a showcase for phenomenal defensive outfielder Duffy Lewis to climb in pursuit of outs (and was thus dubbed "Duffy's Cliff").

A fire in 1926 destroyed a large part of the left-field stands, and a 1934 fire helped ruin much of what was left. But Tom Yawkey, the racehorse-loving Pittsburgh millionaire who had bought the team in 1933 (and who would own it, championship-less, until his death in 1976) was busy making Fenway Park into the perfect palace it is today. Duffy's Cliff was mostly flattened, The Wall rose stronger than before, and the seating was improved.

> **"Fenway Park is the quintessential old-time ballpark. Lovingly called 'that little jewel box of a park' by John Updike, it is more than just a place to watch a ballgame."**

In 1940, the bullpens were moved onto the field in front of the right-field fence, the better for new slugging star Ted Williams to aim his left-handed swing. In 1946, Yawkey put "skyview" seats atop the park's single deck of stands. The only other major renovation came in 1988, when a huge luxury box/press box suite was constructed high above home plate. Many say the park has been sadly affected by this final construction, as its glass-walled hugeness has changed the wind patterns that were so much a part of every game there.

But complaints aside, the park is not very dissimilar to the Elysian field where Williams groused, where Johnny Pesky held the ball, where Tony Conigliaro got beaned, where the Impossible Dream

Following pages: The exterior of Fenway Park in 1912, on a street now known as Yawkey Way.

of 1967 finally did not come true, where Carl Yastrzemski popped up to end a 1978 playoff game with the Yankees, and where nearly a century of Boston fans have left the park each October knowing that for another winter, they were not the champs.

But while the Green Monster in left field (and the annual inability of the Red Sox to bring home a World Series crown) is the big thing that everyone knows about Fenway Park, it's the little things that we love. Here are a few Fenway Park favorites:

• On the left-field scoreboard are two sets of mysterious dots and dashes in vertical rows. Red Sox cognoscenti know that those marks are Morse code for TAY and JRY: Thomas Austin Yawkey and Jean Remington Yawkey, the team's owners from 1933 to 1993.

"The Williams Shift was invented to foil the great hitter, as opposing defenses often rotated their shortstop to play between first and second."

• The flagpole that now stands atop the dead center-field wall was on the field until 1970.

• Fenway Park has two stadium areas named for former players: Williamsburg, the right-field bullpens, after Ted Williams, who deposited multiple homers there, and the Pesky Pole, the right-field foul pole, for shortstop Johnny Pesky, who parked some random dingers around the 302-foot distance.

• In 1966, the team resodded the outfield. Left fielder Carl Yastrzemski had the old sod trucked to his home and put on his lawn.

• Near the top of the green center-field bleachers is one red seat, marking the spot where Ted Williams hit one of his longest homers.

Williams, of course, was a legend in many ways, and his refusal to bend his swing to match Fenway Park is part of his tale.

Left: Hall of Fame outfielder Ted Williams, in the 1940s. **Following pages:** An aerial view of Fenway Park (c. 1993).

Meet the Green Monster

It is the single most famous physical landmark in Major League Baseball, perhaps in all of sports. "The Green Monster" (or simply "The Monster"), as it is commonly known, stands 37 feet tall, a vast, imposing green target for right-handed hitters. You can see the Green Monster on TV, but you can't really understand its impact on the park until you're sitting in the seats. Though it's more than 300 feet away, it seems to rise in front of you as close as a TV screen. It looms. It towers. It overshadows nearly everything else.

"The Wall" (as it was first known) rose in 1912, built to follow Landsdowne Street behind left field. It was made of wooden railroad ties and covered with tin. In 1934, the wood was replaced with sheet metal; two years later, the famous 23-foot screen was put atop the wall to catch homers and to protect cars and buildings. Giant advertisements, most notably for Gem razor blades, were painted on the wall. In 1947, it was painted green. And not just any green, but a trademarked special "Fenway Green." The secret formula for the green is held by the Fenway Painting Company, which got the job serendipitously when the company's name was picked out of the phone book by a team executive looking for a local painter.

The biggest change since '47 came in 2003, when the Red Sox created a set of hotly debated but soon red-hot-popular seats atop the Green Monster. Purists (yours truly included) bemoaned yet another desecration of this beloved monument. But by mid-May the entire season was sold out (save for fifty standing-room-only seats put on sale before every game). Fans raved at the view, the closeness to the action, the scads of home run balls that flew into the seats during batting practice and in the game. ESPN.com's Wayne Drehs sat atop The Wall for a game in May, and all around him, Boston-accented fans on their cell phones reported to their jealous friends, "Dude! I'm on the Monstah!"

Right: No other wall in Major League Baseball even approaches the height of the Green Monster at Fenway Park. The netting above the wall, shown in this picture (c. 2000), was replaced with seating in 2003.

Talented enough to whack any outside pitch he wanted against the Green Monster for an easy hit, he stubbornly kept pulling the ball to right, where his left-handed swing naturally sent the ball. The Williams Shift was invented to foil the great hitter, as opposing defenses often rotated their shortstop to play between first and second. Williams could have bunted safely every time up, but he kept whacking doubles into empty spaces, shift or no shift.

"[Today's] park is not too dissimilar from the Elysian field where Williams groused, where Johnny Pesky held the ball, where Tony Conigliaro got beaned, where the Impossible Dream of 1967 finally did not come true ..."

As much as for his hitting prowess, Williams is well-known for his ongoing feud with the Fenway Park faithful. Peeved at perceived slights early in his career, he never warmed to the fans (and vice versa) and famously never tipped his cap on the field. His final hit in the game was a home run, his 521st, into the right-field seats on September 29, 1960. The event capped his Hall of Fame career with an exclamation point, and gave John Updike the opportunity to write a famous article about the event in *The New Yorker* ("Hub Fans Bid Kid Adieu"). That article, this writer feels, helped begin what would be a decades-long process that turned Williams, "The Splendid Splinter," from irascible star to beloved icon.

In 1999, baseball celebrated the 1900s by naming its All-Century Team. The All-Star Game was held that year at Fenway Park, and dozens of members of that team came to be lauded. At the end, one star remained, and he rode in on a golf cart to cheers and tears. The sight of normally unsentimental big leaguers crowding around the golf cart like Little

Following pages: A day game at Fenway Park (c. 2000).

Magical Moments

April 20, 1912

Fenway Park opens.

June 23, 1917

Ernie Shore takes over after pitcher Babe Ruth is thrown out after
walking the first batter; Shore proceeds to retire 26 batters in a row.

September 11, 1918

The Red Sox defeat the Cubs to win the World Series, the last
championship for the club in the 20th century.

July 9, 1946

Ted Williams blasts Rip Sewell's "eephus" lob pitch for his second
homer as the AL wins the All-Star Game 12-0.

September 29, 1960

Ted Williams hits a homer in his last at-bat.

October 1, 1967

With a 6-3 victory over the Twins, the Red Sox cap the "Impossible
Dream" season by clinching their first AL pennant since 1946.

October 21, 1975

Carlton Fisk's homer in the bottom of the 12th wins
Game 6 of the World Series over the Reds.

October 1, 1983

Yaz Day: Fenway Park honors one
of its heroes—Carl Yastrzemski—on his retirement.

April 29, 1986

Boston's Roger Clemens sets a Major League record by
striking out 20 Seattle Mariners in one game.

July 13, 1999

Pedro Martinez wins the All-Star Game MVP award, while Ted
Williams is the centerpiece of the All-Century Team celebration.

April 24, 2002

Boston's Derek Lowe pitches the first Fenway Park no-hitter since 1965.

Leaguers, just to be near Teddy Ballgame, will remain one of the ball-park's mistiest memories.

The memories of players and teams past remain mental pictures, but the Green Monster in left field (see box) remains the park's (and perhaps the sport's) signature physical landmark. It has played a huge part in some of the most famous moments in Major League Baseball history. Along with Carlton Fisk's homer in 1975 (see page 48), a light-hitting Yankees shortstop parked one in the nets above the Green Monster in 1978 to the continuing devastation of Red Sox fans. That homer won a one-game playoff held after the two teams tied for the AL East crown. To this day, the name of that player can never be uttered by any Boston fan without the use of a word between "Bucky" and "Dent" that is unfit to reprint in a family book.

"Yaz was perhaps the master at deciphering The Wall's idiosyncratic bounces and quirks."

Playing below the wall in left field is one of the game's most unique defensive challenges. From 1939 to 1987, three men, basically, patrolled that swath of green beneath the Green. Ted Williams starred from 1939 to 1960; Carl Yastrzemski from 1961 to 1983; and Jim Rice, from 1975 (when Yaz moved mostly to first base) until 1987, when Rice was more regularly the DH. Yaz was perhaps the master at deciphering The Wall's idiosyncratic bounces and quirks. Hours of practice at learning how a ball bounced off helped him win eight Gold Glove awards and regularly turn long whacks off The Wall from doubles into singles. He could tell from the sound of the ball hitting the wall whether it would rebound out toward the field (*thump*) or down toward the warning track (*twink*). More than once he decoyed an unsuspecting hitter into thinking that the ball was heading for the netting, only to run into an out as Yaz grabbed the rebound and fired

Right: Boston's Hall of Fame outfielder Carl Yastrzemski, or "Yaz," in 1979.

Waving at History

On the long list of Major League moments known by a shorthand recognizable to all loyal fans is this: Fisk. Mention the name of Red Sox catcher Carlton Fisk and the first thing that comes to every fan's mind is a soggy October evening in 1975. Fenway Park was not only the setting, but also one of the stars of what is often regarded as the greatest game ever played.

The Red Sox trailed the Cincinnati Reds in the World Series, three games to two. A win by the Reds would once again send the Red Sox home for a long, sad winter. The action was epic—the game went back-and-forth as the two teams traded clutch hits. Bernie Carbo's pinch-hit, three-run homer tied the game in the eighth. The Reds cut down Boston's potential winning run at the plate in the ninth. Boston's Dwight Evans stole a home run from Joe Morgan in the 11th with a catch at the right-field bullpen fence. And then came Fisk.

As the clock neared midnight, Fisk led off the 12th inning. He slugged the second pitch he saw toward The Wall in left field. NBC's TV cameras stayed on Fisk as he hopped down the first-base line, waving, waving, waving, coaxing the ball fair as it rose into the dark. It was fair. The hops turned to leaps, the Boston faithful erupted, and the game was over.

Of course, this being the cursed Red Sox, they lost Game 7 at home to the Reds, continuing their 20th-century futility in the Fall Classic.

the ball into second. Yaz and other left fielders also had to contend with a ladder that for many years let ground crew members ascend to the netting to retrieve baseballs. It was the only ladder in play in the Majors. Finally, the field-level scoreboard (hand-operated from inside a tiny field-level room) can make the ball change direction faster than George Steinbrenner can fire managers.

Knowledge of the park is essential to success. Generations of Red Sox shortstops have learned to head toward left field on balls hit sharply down the third-base line. They are there to protect against a sometimes-wacky hop off the stands that jut out toward the foul line. And Red Sox base runners know to take advantage of visiting shortstops who forget this duty. The strange triangle of space formed by the right-field bullpens and the center-field fence in the deepest part of the park also causes problems. A ball hit to that area can be a double or a home run, the difference decided by the width of a yellow line painted on the wall. And knowledgeable right fielders know that the short wall in front of the bullpens can be useful—they can easily reach over this low wall to snag potential homers.

Besides its on-field quirks, Fenway Park offers one of the game's most wonderful fan experiences in the stands. Yes, the place still smells like beer from 1946, but walking around Fenway Park on game day remains one of the game's loveliest thrills. The sights and sounds are endless: the peanut vendors on Yawkey Way, the crowds surrounding the will-call at Gate A, the lines of souvenir and sausage vendors, the police on horseback, the rattle of Boston accents, the high brick walls with the "1912" plaque at the top, the Green Monster rising up above Ted Williams Way (what was formerly Landsdowne Street).

> **"The Fenway Park experience is not one that should only be read about—it should also be experienced in person, and savored in memory forever."**

More words have been written about Fenway Park and its charms and history than probably any other park. What is written here is mere summation. The Fenway Park experience is not one that should only be read about—it should also be experienced in person, and savored in memory forever.

Following pages: Outside Fenway Park on game day (1996), Yawkey Way is a sea of Red Sox fans.

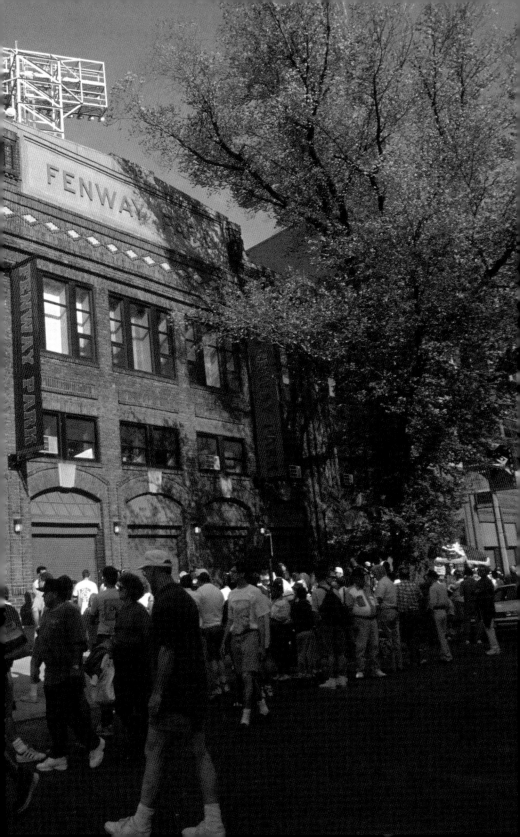

Chapter Three

TIGER
STADIUM

ctually, this chapter title is only partly appropriate. The former home of the Detroit Tigers at the corner of Michigan and Trumbull in Motor City was born in 1912 as Navin Field. From 1938 to 1960 it was Briggs Stadium. It was only Tiger Stadium for the final thirty-eight years of its life. To be even more precise, another park at that famous corner preceded Navin Field. Known as Bennett Field (see box, page 64), it was the den of the Tigers from 1896 to 1911. (A bit of trivia for you: Bennett Field was named for a former Tigers catcher who lost his feet in an 1893 train accident. Charlie Bennett caught the ceremonial first pitch at every Tigers home opener from 1901 to 1926.) In fact, until the Tigers left this address after the 1999 season, Michigan and Trumbull was the oldest continuously used site in any major sport.

While at Bennett Field, team owners battled with landowners along National and Cherry Streets outside the park who built "wildcat" bleachers. The Tigers didn't see a dime from these out-side seats, and often put up large canvas sheets to try to block the views. Of course, this just led the landowners to build higher bleachers. Eventually the fire marshal stepped in and closed the bleachers down (for the most part).

....

Following pages: Before 1960, Detroit's ballpark was called Briggs Stadium, which was in turn preceded by Navin Field (1912–1938) and Bennett Field (1896–1911). The ballpark is shown here in the 1930s.

....

TIGER STADIUM

Ballpark Basics

Location: Detroit, corner of Michigan and Trumbull

Date opened: April 20, 1912

Approximate cost: $300,000

Tenants: Detroit Tigers, 1912–1999

Outfield distances: Left field: 340 feet; Left-center field: 365 feet; Center field: 440 feet; Right-center field: 375 feet; Right field: 325 feet.

Largest crowd: 58,480, May 19, 1946

Capacity: 52,416

Home team W-L record: Detroit Tigers at home (1912–1999): 3,764-3,090

First home run: Del Pratt, St. Louis Browns (May 5, 1912)

Last home run: Robert Fick, Detroit Tigers (September 27, 1999)

Player with most home runs: Al Kaline, Detroit Tigers (226)

Number of no-hit games pitched (and most recent): 8 (Nolan Ryan, California Angels vs. Detroit Tigers, July 15, 1973)

Other events/sports: Hosted Major League Baseball All-Star Game in 1941, 1951, and 1971 . . . Home to three pro football teams, including the NFL's Detroit Lions from 1940 to 1974.

Unusual ground rules: A 125-foot flag pole in deep center field was in play...In two seasons (1944 and 1961), a screen over the lower deck in right field meant that balls had to be hit into the upper deck to be home runs.

In 1912, Tigers owner Frank Navin finally shut down the wildcats for good while at the same time creating the footprint for the park that would be the team's home for almost 90 years. He spent $300,000 (estimated at $50 million in today's dollars) to create a single-deck park that seated 23,000. The concrete-and-steel "U" behind home plate was covered along both baselines. In deep right-center field, he also built wooden bleacher seats. Hall of Fame outfielder Ty Cobb helped christen the new park, known as Navin Field, by stealing home in the first inning.

Though there were few other on-field highlights for the home team in the next two decades, the fans kept coming to the little park. Detroit led the AL in attendance in 1919, and in 1924 became only the second AL team (after the Yankees) to top one million fans in a season. That latter mark was boosted by the addition in 1923 of a second deck to the grandstand behind home plate. (In the very

Above: Hall of Famer Ty Cobb, shown here in 1910, still holds many batting records.

The Other Stars of Detroit

Several other professional baseball teams made their homes at Navin Field. From 1920 to 1937, the Detroit Stars and Detroit Wolves of the Negro National and American Leagues, respectively, played there, often to big crowds. (Of the parks featured in this book, Yankee Stadium and Ebbets Field were also the sites of Negro League games.)

Hall of Fame outfielder Turkey Stearnes starred for Detroit, and fans were able to see visiting heroes such as Josh Gibson, Satchel Paige, and Judy Johnson. None of them played in the Major Leagues, however, and none of them ever faced the Tigers in a game that counted (offseason exhibition games were common between Negro League and Major League teams and players). The Negro Leagues were the only way that African-American players (or black Cubans or Dominicans) could play pro ball in the United States at that time. They played in Major League stadiums. They dressed in Major League locker rooms. They played a caliber of ball that was often, if not always, the equal of Major League action—even if they were not recognized for this. The Negro Leagues finally faded into history in the mid-1950s, as the barrier broken by Jackie Robinson in 1947 (see page 69) opened the way to African-American players, who integrated the Majors.

detailed book about the ballpark, *A Place for Summer*, by Richard Bak, there is a photo of workmen filling the empty seats with sandbags to test the strength of the new structure.) In 1934, the fans' loyalty was rewarded when future Hall of Fame catcher Mickey Cochrane arrived as player-manager to spark some of the team's best seasons.

Cochrane was joined by future Hall of Famers Charlie Gehringer, Hank Greenberg, and Goose Goslin, and together they helped Detroit to a 101-53 record (that .656 winning percentage remains a club record). Though the club lost in Game 7 of the 1934 World Series to the Cardinals, they stormed back in 1935 to win their first World Series title. Sadly, Navin died a month after the Series ended.

In 1936, Walter Briggs took over the team and promptly spent more than a million dollars fixing up the park again. Briggs' additions created the ballpark that fans would enjoy for

Above: Hall of Fame first baseman Hank Greenberg (shown here in 1945) gave up five years of his career to serve in World War II and was a hero to many—especially fellow Jewish-Americans.

Gibson's First Classic Clout

Kirk Gibson will forever be a part of baseball legend for the home run he hit for the Dodgers in Game 1 of the 1988 World Series. Hobbling and appearing only as a pinch-hitter, he whacked a 3-2 slider off Oakland's ace reliever Dennis Eckersley to win the game. But that was not the first historic Series homer Gibson hit.

In 1984, the former Michigan State All-American wide receiver was a slugging outfielder for the Tigers. That season's Detroit team was one of the most dominant of recent decades, busting out to a 35-5 start and leading from wire to wire. They romped through the playoffs and led the San Diego Padres three games to one in the World Series.

In Game 5, at a packed and roaring Tiger Stadium, Gibson put on a show. He smacked homers into the upper deck in right field in the first and eighth innings, for a total of five RBI. He also scored in the fifth to break a 3-3 tie, charging home from third on a short sacrifice fly like he was bulling for the end zone.

It was the first title for the Tigers since 1968 and their last through 2003. A sad coda to the night came when the post-game celebration got out of hand and pictures of burning police cars outside Tiger Stadium were seen around the world. The scene helped fuel the growing urge among civic leaders to create a newer, "nicer" place for the Tigers to prowl.

Right: Slugger Kirk Gibson led an exceptional 1984 Tigers team to a World Series Championship.

another 60-plus years. He continued the double-decking all the way around the park, to make the only fully enclosed two-deck park in the Majors at that time. Seating capacity rose to 53,000, and a wonderful quirk was established in right field. To accommodate the double-decking, designers extended the top deck about 10 feet over the playing field. A high fly ball that would have been caught at the wall could now be snagged by a fan in one of those seats, creating a pretty cheap home run. The bullpens, meanwhile, were moved to center field, scoreboards were added to outfield walls, and the largest press box in the Majors was built high above home plate.

"Detroit led the AL in attendance in 1919, and in 1924 became only the second AL team (after the Yankees) to top one million fans in a season."

As a lifelong fan, Briggs saw his dream of team ownership come true. He continually worked to make his ballpark a showplace, painting the seats annually and using a tarp made of new-fangled nylon to protect the field during rain delays.

In 1939, the building was the scene of one of the saddest days in Major League Baseball. After 2,130 consecutive games, Yankees great Lou Gehrig, the "Iron Horse," took himself out of the lineup before a game against the Tigers. The poignant photo of Gehrig sitting on the Briggs Stadium dugout steps watching the game instead of playing presaged the end of one the sport's greatest careers. He died two years later of ALS, the disease that now bears his name (see box, page 120).

After losing again in the World Series in 1940, the Tigers returned to the top in 1945. Greenberg returned from five years of Army service to star again, clubbing a grand slam in the final game to clinch the pennant. They knocked off the Cubs in the World Series, with pitcher Hal Newhouser winning league MVP honors.

Magical Moments

April 20, 1912

Detroit's Ty Cobb inaugurates the new ballpark on opening day by stealing home in the first inning.

October 9, 1934

Tigers fans pelt Cardinals outfielder Joe Medwick with garbage during St. Louis' 11-0 World Series-clinching win.

October 7, 1935

Tigers defeat the Cubs to capture their first World Series title.

May 2, 1939

Lou Gehrig voluntarily ends his record consecutive games streak of 2,130.

July 8, 1941

Ted Williams blasts a three-run homer to win the All-Star Game for the AL.

July 13, 1971

Reggie Jackson of the Athletics crashes a massive homer off the light tower atop the right-field seats as the AL wins the All-Star Game 6-4.

October 14, 1984

Detroit's Kirk Gibson homers twice as the Tigers beat the Padres 8-4 to win the World Series title.

April 20, 1988

Detroit fans gather to give Tiger Stadium a "group hug" in an unsuccessful effort to save the park.

August 25, 1990

Detroit's Cecil Fielder becomes one of only three players to hit a homer over the left-field roof.

September 27, 1999

Final game played at Tiger Stadium.

Before the Stadium

In 1896, the Detroit franchise in the Western League moved to a ballfield that had been home to a haymarket. The owners covered the old cobblestones of the market with topsoil, giving infielders a ready excuse for an error: "It hit a cobblestone." The team spruced things up by 1901 when it joined the new American League, adding bleachers and nicer seating, though the crowd still often spilled into the outfield, even into fair territory.

Though the fancier Navin Field would replace this old place in 1912, Bennett Field was witness to some wonderful baseball. Perhaps the biggest highlight came in Detroit's very first AL game, April 25, 1901. The hometown fans were disappointed when their local heroes entered the bottom of the ninth trailing Milwaukee 13-4. But anyone who stuck around saw the greatest last-inning comeback in Major League history, as the Tigers scored 10 runs, including four with two outs, to win 14-13.

They would not reach the top again until 1968, and again in 1984 (see box, page 60). Meanwhile, in 1961, Briggs Stadium was renamed Tiger Stadium. But for Tigers fans, the biggest news of the past few decades has not been the team's annually abysmal record, but the closing of their beloved ballpark.

It was a long and drawn-out death, with rounds of proposals for renovation and promises from several owners never to close the park. Fans around the country rallied to try to save the place, going so far as to give the old yard a group hug in 1988. More than 1,200 people encircled Tiger Stadium with hands linked to show some love. Love, however, lost out to commerce and typically-convoluted Detroit politics. City officials claimed the old park was falling down, though independent engineers told a different story. Estimates for the cost of renovations rose and fell depending on who was doing the accounting. A fans' group even got the place put on the National Register of Historic Places. It was, however, to no avail.

The last game in Tiger Stadium was played on September 27, 1999. The Tigers knocked off the Royals 8-2, but the game hardly mattered. Post-game ceremonies included dozens of former Tigers notables, from Al Kaline to Gates Brown, from Alan Trammell and Lou Whitaker to relatives of Charlie Bennett and Walter Briggs.

Kaline spoke for generations of fans and players during a pregame ceremony. "The Tiger Stadium experience is about so much more than winning and losing. It is a bond that all the people of Detroit share. Tiger Stadium's strength lies not in dazzling architecture or creature comforts, but rather in character, charm, and history. While common materials may have been used to build this place, the memories are the cement that has held it together for 88 wonderful seasons."

After the game, flags were lowered, tears were shed, and home plate was dug up and transported about a mile away to what would become Comerica Park. The lights were dimmed, one bank at a time. Longtime broadcaster Ernie Harwell gave the final benediction. And that was that.

Comerica Park is now the place where the Detroit Tigers play, but for millions of fans, the home of the Tigers will always be at the corner of Michigan and Trumbull.

"Fans around the country rallied to try to save the place, going so far as to give the old yard a group hug in 1988. More than 1,200 people encircled Tiger Stadium with hands linked to show some love."

Following pages: The Tigers play the Toronto Blue Jays at Tiger Stadium, June 19, 1994.

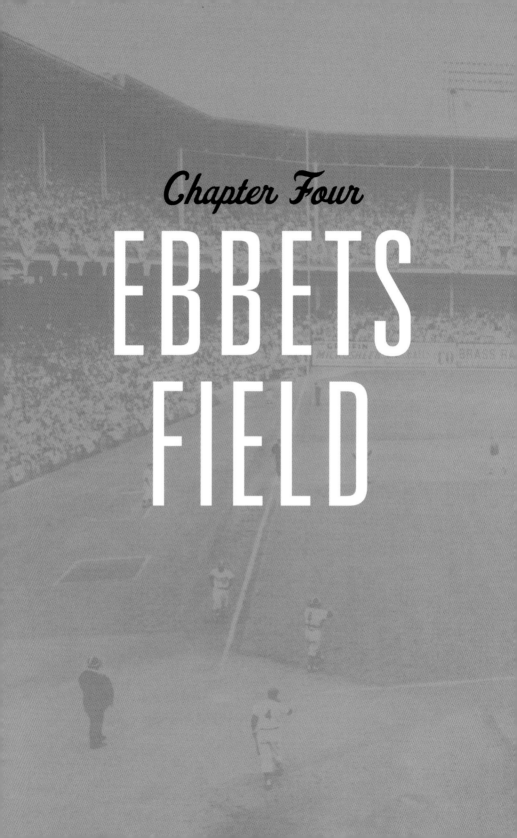

Chapter Four

EBBETS FIELD

t could be argued, and in fact has been argued, by sports fans and non–sports fans alike, that the most significant moment in the 20th century occurred on a baseball diamond. Since the earliest days of the American republic, the relationship between people of European descent and those of African descent has been one of almost constant turmoil and abuse. Though far from perfect today, relations between the "races" have advanced light years, and many people point to a moment in 1947 as the tipping point, the "hinge" in history when everything changed forever. But what does that have to do with a ballpark?

Well, on April 15, 1947, in Ebbets Field in the borough of Brooklyn in the city of New York, an African-American man played Major League Baseball. Jackie Robinson was the Brooklyn Dodgers first baseman that day, the first African-American player ever in the Majors. It was a glorious day in a glorious place.

Thirty-four years before that momentous day, on April 9, 1913, a former office clerk named Charles Ebbets had seen his dream realized and a new ballpark opened in a place that used to be known as Pigtown, not far from Prospect Park in Brooklyn. Ebbets, who had risen from team accountant to team owner, had quietly bought up land in the area from several hundred small landowners, disclosing his plans for a ballpark only toward the end of that process. Though Pigtown was essentially a garbage

---

Following pages: Jackie Robinson steals home in the 1953 World Series.

EBBETS FIELD

Ballpark Basics

Location: Brooklyn, New York, corner of McKeever St. and Sullivan Ave.

Date opened: April 9, 1913

Approximate cost: $750,000

Tenants: Brooklyn Dodgers, 1913–1957

Outfield distances: Left field: 350 feet; Left-center field: 351 feet; Center field: 393 feet (since 1955); Right-center field: 352 feet; Right field: 297 feet

Largest crowd: 41,209, May 30, 1934

Capacity: 31,000–35,000

Home team W-L record: Brooklyn Dodgers at home (1913–1957): 1,964-1,450

First home run: Casey Stengel, Brooklyn Dodgers (April 26, 1913)

Last home run: Duke Snider, Brooklyn Dodgers (November 22, 1957)

Player with most home runs: Duke Snider, Brooklyn Dodgers (224)

Number of no-hit games pitched (and most recent): 7 (Sal Maglie, Brooklyn Dodgers vs. Philadelphia Phillies, September 25, 1956)

Other events/sports: Hosted Major League Baseball All-Star Game in 1949 . . . Home to several professional football teams, including the NFL's Brooklyn Dodgers (1930–1943) and the AAFC's Brooklyn Dodgers (1946–1948) . . . Site of the first televised pro football game in 1939 (between the NFL's Brooklyn Dodgers and Philadelphia Eagles).

Unusual ground rules: Balls hit into the 19-foot screen atop the right-field wall were in play.

dump, it was located in a propitious place, near the nexus of several trolley lines and subway routes. (As most fans can tell you, those trolleys were the source of the team's name. Brooklynites were known as Trolley Dodgers for their death-defying dashes through traffic of cars, trolleys, horses, and more.) Ebbets Field was a real urban ballpark, with parking for only seven hundred cars even in its heyday.

The park that Ebbets put up was a mix of the palatial and the plain. The rotunda through which fans entered behind home plate was a thing of baseball beauty. The floor had tiles forming the stitching of a baseball. A huge chandelier rose above the gilded ticket cages, made of dozens of crossed bats.

> "Charles Ebbets had seen his dream realized and a new ballpark opened in a place that used to be known as Pigtown, not far from Prospect Park in Brooklyn."

Inside the place was less grand. It was the quintessential bandbox of a ballpark, with fans hovering next to the field well within shouting distance. Foul ground was sparse, and the bullpens were right along the short walls holding back the fans (though the walls could not hold back their vociferous cheering and jeering).

The initial park held 18,000. In 1926 more bleachers were added, while a double-deck was added in 1931 from third base to left-center field. Capacity increased to 35,000, and the place that author Michael Gershman writes was a "shrine to Brooklynness" assumed its final, famous shape.

Few parks have ever created a tighter bond between fans and team than did Ebbets Field. Through the years that the "Bums" played in front of them, Brooklyn's fans became almost as well known

Following pages: The famous rotunda entrance to Ebbets Field, shown here circa 1914, before cars filled the streets of Brooklyn.

as the players. Among the most well known was Hilda Chester, a grand-motherly woman who rang her cowbell and bellowed for her boys. Jack Pierce cheered for outfielder Cookie Lavagetto. Pierce's piercing "Cooooookie!" cry echoed through the park, while Pierce let go balloons with his hero's name on them. A man known only as Albie the Truck Driver christened the team with its famous moniker. He even turned down a season pass to the park, offered as incentive to go easy on the boys, for the chance to continue his harangues against "Da Bums."

The most noted of the Ebbets Field denizens were the members of the "Dodgers Sym-phoney," made up originally of several fans who came together independently to serenade Dodgers and visitors alike. They got so popular that the team organized them and gave them permanent seats. Gershman tells the story of the time that the local musicians' union demanded that the musical group be paid. They threatened to picket, but owner Walter O'Malley instead invited everyone to come to that game with an instrument of any kind. It was too much for the union, and they relented.

These fans bestowed decades of love on their team, along with an encyclopedia's worth of famous nicknames: Pistol Pete Reiser, Pee Wee Reese, Duke Snider, and Shotgun Shuba. Carl Furillo earned a pair: Skoonj, for his beloved scungilli, and the Reading Rifle, for his awesome throwing arm.

> **"Few parks have ever created a tighter bond between fans and team than did Ebbets Field. Through the years that the 'Bums' played in front of them, Brooklyn's fans became almost as well known as the players."**

Left: Infielder Pee Wee Reese, pictured here in the 1950s, was one of many Dodgers stars given a nickname by devoted Brooklyn fans. **Following pages:** Hitting the Abe Stark sign at the base of the Ebbets Field scoreboard won batters a free suit (shown here in 1957).

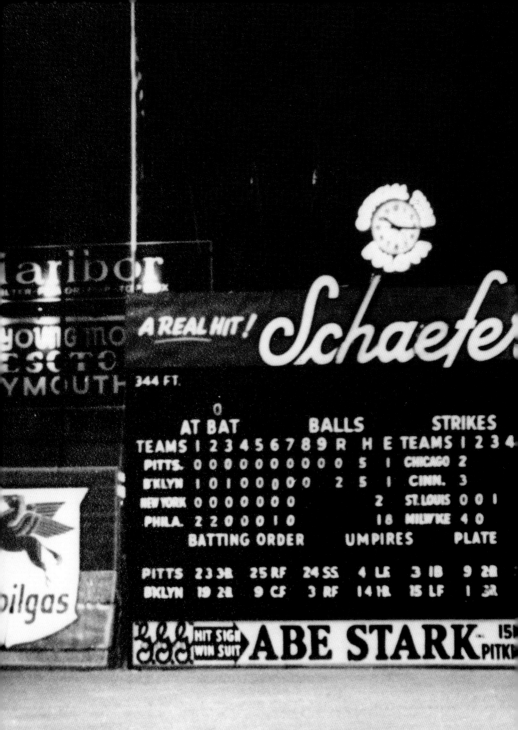

Ebbets Field boasted some of the most famous outfield-wall advertisements ever, as well. At the bottom of the right-field wall was a sign that read "Hit Sign. Win Suit." Clothier Abe Stark made the offer, but didn't pay up as often as one might think, given the distance to the sign. The Schaefer Beer sign above the right-field scoreboard played a role in the game; the "h" and "e" letters in the sign lit up to signal whether a play was a hit or an error.

Throughout their time at Ebbets Field, the Dodgers were rarely contenders. One rare successful period came when they won NL pennants in 1916 and 1920, led by manager Wilbert Robinson. Robinson was so identified with the team that for a while they were known as the Robins. Not until 1941, however, did the team return to the World Series. Even then, they were ill-fated, and their downfall came at Ebbets Field.

"The park that Ebbets put up was a mix of the palatial and the plain."

The Dodgers trailed the Yankees two games to one. In Game 4, they led 4-3 in the ninth. Tommy Henrich struck out for what should have been the final out, tying the World Series at two games apiece. Instead, Brooklyn catcher Mickey Owen let the ball get away from him, and Henrich reached first. The floodgates opened, the Yankees scored four runs with two outs, and they never looked back, winning the World Series in five games.

The period after World War II was the heyday of the Dodgers and Ebbets Field. The team won five NL pennants in 10 years (1947–1956) and was consistently among the top teams in the NL. Another New York team, however, had their number. The Dodgers lost to the Yankees in the Series in 1947, 1949, 1952, and 1953, and the cry of "wait 'til next year" was heard throughout the borough almost every October.

When the Dodgers beat the Yankees in the World Series in 1955, their long-awaited "next year" was finally there. Johnny

Dodgers on the Air

Dodgers fans who couldn't make it to Ebbets Field enjoyed hearing one of the finest radio announcers of all time. From his self-proclaimed "catbird seat," Red Barber called Dodgers games from 1939 to 1953. His folksy and yet pointed commentary was a fixture of the game. Among many things, Red was famous for his three-minute egg timer; he made sure to give the score of the game every time its sands ran out. In 1978, Barber was the first winner (along with Mel Allen) of the Ford C. Frick Award, given annually to top broadcasters by the National Baseball Hall of Fame.

While Red made his name on the radio, he was also part of an important first at Ebbets Field. On August 26, 1939, the Dodgers home game against the Cincinnati Reds became the first Major League Baseball game broadcast on television. The signal was limited and could be seen only by the several hundred sets in the New York area. But it was the start of an era that would dramatically change not only the business, but the perception of the sport by Americans. World Series games are all at night now, to find home-bound audiences. The rights fees paid by networks have played a big part in the game's expansion. And it all started at Ebbets Field.

Podres pitched a 2-0 shutout in Game 7, sparking a celebration that would last, some might argue, to this day. Parades ran down Flatbush Avenue, a slightly shabby borough had its day, and good old Brooklyn was "da champs."

Sadly, within three years, Ebbets Field was empty. O'Malley had been trying to find a way to get a better stadium throughout most of the decade, looking at other sites in Brooklyn. In 1956, trolley lines

Following pages: Ebbets Field, during the momentous 1955 World Series.

WRIGLEY FIELD

Ballpark Basics

Location: 1060 W. Addison Street, Chicago

Date opened: April 23, 1914

Approximate cost: $250,000

Tenants: Chicago Cubs, 1914–present

Outfield distances: Left field: 355 feet; Left-center field: 357 feet; Center field: 400 feet; Right-center field: 363 feet; Right field: 353 feet

Largest crowd: 51,556, June 27, 1930

Capacity (2003): 39,241

Home team W-L record: Chicago Cubs at home (1914–present) 3,751-3,277 (through 2003)

First home run: Johnny Beall, Cincinnati Reds (April 20, 1916)

Last home run: not applicable

Player with most home runs: Ernie Banks, Chicago Cubs (290)

Number of no-hit games pitched (and most recent): 8 (Milt Pappas, Chicago Cubs vs. San Diego Padres, September 2, 1972)

Other events/sports: Hosted Major League Baseball All-Star Game in 1947, 1962, and 1990 . . . Home to several pro football teams, including the Chicago Bears and the Chicago Cardinals at the same time in the 1930s . . . The Bears made their home here from 1922 to 1970.

Unusual ground rules: Player who hits a fair ball that is lost in the ivy that grows along the outfield walls is awarded a ground-rule double . . . A screen that measured 8 feet high by 64 feet wide stood atop the center-field fence from midway through the 1963 season through the 1964 season. It was considered in play and prevented several home runs . . . A basket that was built atop the outfield wall in 1970 extends over the playing field. Any ball hit into the basket is a home run.

Weeghman had made his fortune by trying new things in the restaurant business, and he kept it up in the baseball biz. His park was the first where fans could keep foul balls hit into the stands (in more recent seasons, Chicago's outfield bleacher denizens started another tradition followed in some parks of throwing back home run balls hit by opposing hitters—though potentially valuable balls are usually kept). Weeghman's food-service experience also led him to create the first built-in concession areas (in addition to the by-then-traditional vendors roving the stands).

When the Federal League broke up before the 1916 season, National League owners made sure that, suddenly, all was forgiven and invited Weeghman to buy a franchise in the established NL. They knew a good ballpark when they saw one and wanted to make sure that the Northside kept hopping. The franchise Weeghman bought was the Cubs, who were, way back then before Sammy Sosa was a glimmer in Harry Caray's eye, a pretty decent club. They were the World Series champs in 1908 (their final World Series championship title of the century, it would turn out), had played in the World Series as recently as 1910, and would win an NL title again in 1918.

In 1916 they moved into Weeghman Field (before that they played mostly at DePaul University). In 1918 Weeghman was forced by business losses away from the ballpark to sell his team; the buyer was William Wrigley Jr., of the famous chewing-gum family. Wrigley soon put his stamp on the park, undertaking a major renovation that by 1926 increased capacity to more than 38,000. The park took on its current, gum-inspired name that same year; the exact origins of its best-known nickname, "The Friendly Confines," are murkier.

From the moment he took over, William Wrigley made it his mission to make his ballpark a special place for fans. "I spent $2,300,000 to make Wrigley Field clean, convenient, comfortable, and attractive to

---

Following page: Cubs slugger Sammy Sosa, shown here in 2002.

Magical Moments

May 2, 1917

The only double no-hit game in Major League Baseball history is pitched by Jim "Hippo" Vaughn of the Cubs and Fred Toney of the Cincinnati Reds. Toney wins in the 10th when Jim Thorpe hits a homer off Vaughn.

October 1, 1932

Babe Ruth of the Yankees "calls" his home run against Cubs pitcher Charlie Root in Game 5 of the 1932 World Series.

September 28, 1938

As darkness is falling over Wrigley Field, Gabby Hartnett hits "The Homer in the Gloamin'," to win a key late-season game against Pittsburgh.

October 10, 1945

The Cubs lose to Detroit in their final World Series appearance of the 20th century.

May 12, 1970

Ernie Banks hits his 500th career homer.

September 8, 1985

Cincinnati's Pete Rose ties Ty Cobb's all-time hits record at 4,191.

April 9, 1988

First official night game is played at Wrigley Field.

July 10, 1990

The first nighttime All-Star Game in Wrigley history (and first at the park since 1962) is won by the AL 2-0.

April 4, 1994

Cubs rookie Tuffy Rhodes hits three solo homers on opening day, but the Cubs lose 12-8.

May 6, 1998

Cubs rookie Kerry Wood ties a single-game record by striking out 20 Houston Astros.

the eye," he said. "The effect of these improved surroundings upon baseball patrons has been remarkable."

He passed that mission on to his son, Philip K. Wrigley, who took over after his father died in 1932. Philip Wrigley set out to make the ballpark a showplace (though some would grouse that he paid more attention to the park than to the team). In 1937, Bill Veeck, then a Cubs executive but later one of the most famous innovators as a team owner, helped install the center-field scoreboard, still hand-operated today. The huge round clock atop the scoreboard went in at the same time. Later that year, Philip Wrigley ordered trees to be added to the park to beautify it. Someone forgot to tell the fierce Lake Michigan winds and, according to Veeck, the leaves were stripped in a day. More successful was the installation that season of pots of ivy to grow up the brick outfield wall. That more-hardy plant took with vigor and today remains the park's signature sight. No other park can boast such verdant charms; of course, in no other park can a ball get lost in the ivy (it's a ground-rule double).

This era in the ballpark's history saw it bear witness to a string of legendary moments. Here is a sampling:

"From the moment he took over, William Wrigley made it his mission to make his ballpark a special place for fans."

• May 2, 1917: The only double no-hit game in Major League Baseball history was pitched. Chicago's Jim "Hippo" Vaughn pitched nine innings without allowing a hit; Cincinnati's Fred Toney went him one better by tossing 10 such innings. The Reds won it in the 10th on a homer by none other than double-Olympic-gold-medalist Jim Thorpe.

• October 1, 1932: Babe Ruth's "Called Shot." In Game 5 of the

Left: Before 1937, the Wrigley Field outfield walls were bare brick, without their signature ivy coating (shown here in 1996). **Following pages:** A day game at Wrigley Field, 1996, with the Cubs playing the Atlanta Braves.

1932 World Series, Ruth stepped up against Chicago's Charlie Root. With two strikes against him, Ruth did something that is debated to this day: He gestured in some fashion. Many contend he was pointing to the center-field seats. Others say he was pointing to Root. Still others say he was motioning to the hecklers on the Chicago bench. What is not debated is what he did next: wallop a typically Ruthian blast to dead center field. Did he "call" his homer? As Babe once said, "It makes a hell of a story, doesn't it?"

> "Ernie Banks put on a prodigious power display, smacking 512 career homers and winning back-to-back MVP awards in 1958 and 1959, two of the few ever given to a player on a last-place team."

• September 28, 1938: "The Homer in the Gloamin'." With darkness falling and the Cubs trailing in a key late-season game against Pittsburgh, catcher Gabby Hartnett slugged a homer that disappeared into the misty twilight. Did it go out? Did fans reach out to pull it into their loving embrace? Hartnett touched home, and days later, the Cubs brought home the NL pennant to Wrigley Field.

• 1945: The last World Series appearance for the Cubs in the 20th century. They lost. In the years since, the level of Cubs fans' love for Wrigley Field has risen in direct proportion to their team's distance from the World Series. The ivy has grown steadily while the Cubs have just as steadily avoided the Major League Baseball Fall Classic. Though the grand old place has seen some of the game's greatest and most beloved personalities, the Cubs have unfortunately also created a legend as lovable losers.

In the 1950s and 1960s, Wrigley Field faithful watched shortstop/first baseman Ernie Banks put on a prodigious power display,

---

Right: Cubs shortstop/first baseman Ernie Banks, in the 1950s . **Following pages:** Though some things have changed over the years, Wrigley Field (shown here in 1996) remains a special place for fans.

Harry and the Bleacher Bums

No discussion of Wrigley Field is complete without a paean to the late Harry Caray, the beloved Cubs broadcaster from 1982 until his death in 1998. After a long career with the rival Cardinals, Caray was immediately a hit in Chicago with his Everyman style and quickly became as much a part of the place as the ivy. Sporting his trademark enormous eyeglasses, Caray would broadcast some games while sitting shirtless in the outfield bleachers. And he became a national icon for, among other things, leading the crowd from his announcers' booth in singing *Take Me Out to the Ballgame* during the seventh-inning stretch. In Harry's memory, to this day, a parade of celebrity guests continues the tradition, with everyone from Bill Murray to Dick Butkus giving it the old Caray try. Cubs fans from coast to coast still miss his famous game-ending call, "Cubs win! Cubs win!"

Right: Energetic Cubs announcer Harry Caray, shown here circa 1996, always led the fans in singing the traditional "Take Me Out to the Ballgame."

smacking 512 career homers and winning back-to-back MVP awards in 1958 and 1959, two of the few ever given to a player on a last-place team. Banks, of course, is one of the sport's true gentlemen, whose enthusiasm for the game is most famously heard in his classic suggestion: "It's such a nice day, let's play two." Of course, when you play half your games in such a lovely place, that's not hard to consider.

The way that some fans, for many years, enjoyed watching those games has also gone somewhat by the boards. Behind the

right-field fence on Sheffield Avenue, enterprising property owners would charge friends and neighbors a few bucks to stand on their apartment house roofs and watch the game. From there, you could see all the way to home plate, though the bleachers directly in front of you cut off some of the outfield. The mini-bleachers (like the wildcat stands built by Tigers fans; see page 53) became a big hit and grew quickly in popularity. Not surprisingly, laws and money soon interceded. In the 1990s, the Cubs put up screens that blocked some sightlines, while the city mandated permits for other buildings. You can still sit up there, but now you can buy your ticket online and it's not as seat-of-the-pants as it used to be.

One of the other unique things about Wrigley Field is that until 1988, whether Ernie was playing one or two in a day, all games were played then: in the day. Wrigley Field was the last park in the bigs to add lights and play night games. Crosley Field in Cincinnati was the first in 1938, and by 1948 all the other parks had followed suit (Detroit's Briggs Stadium was the last save for Wrigley Field to install lights). Ironically, Wrigley Field had lights ready to go up before the 1942 season. Construction was set for December 8, 1941, but following Pearl Harbor, the steel for the light towers was donated to the war effort and the lights stayed out.

The "fight" to add lights to Wrigley Field was sparked by some rare Cubs success. In 1984, the club made the NL Championship Series, one step from the World Series. Though the Cubs lost that series to San Diego, Major League Baseball made it clear that future playoff games involving the Cubs would be played at night. The team worked for four years to overturn local ordinances against night baseball and to assuage legions of

Following pages: An aerial view of Wrigley Field (c. 1993) shows fans gathered on nearby rooftops (bottom left, center) catching views of the ballgame.

The Goat's Revenge

The Chicago Cubs have gone longer than any other Major League team without winning a championship. Their most recent World Series title came in 1908 . . . they haven't even made it to the World Series since 1945! Three times, however, they have come achingly close, and the Wrigley Field faithful have witnessed not the celebrations they so craved, but instead three of the game's biggest chokes. Some say those chokes are because of a goat.

In 1969 the Cubs boasted one of their most powerful teams. Ernie Banks, Ron Santo, and Billy Williams led on the field, while veteran manager Leo Durocher pulled the strings. The Cubs roared all summer and by August 13, they were in first place by nine-and-a-half games. About two weeks later, stunningly, the Mets were in first and the Cubs in second. Then, to make things worse, from September 2 through 11, the Cubs lost eight straight, while the Mets won 10 straight. That was that, and the Cubs watched the playoffs on TV.

In 1984, Chicago won the NL East division behind MVP Ryne Sandberg and pitching ace Rick Sutcliffe. The Cubs won the first two games of the NL Championship Series at Wrigley Field, and the World Series was but one win away. Almost inevitably, the Padres won three straight games in San Diego, and the Cubs were losers again.

In 2003, it was not a goat, but a fan who continued the cursed history of the Cubs. On their way to a seeming victory at Wrigley Park in Game 6 of the NLCS against the Florida Marlins, Chicago was derailed again. With the Cubs just five outs away from a trip to the Fall Classic, a fan reaching out for a foul ball knocked it away from Chicago outfielder Moises Alou, letting the Marlins keep their momentum during an eight-run eighth inning. The Cubs lost that game, and then lost Game 7 (though they led that game 5-3 in the third), thus keeping their World Series–free streak alive.

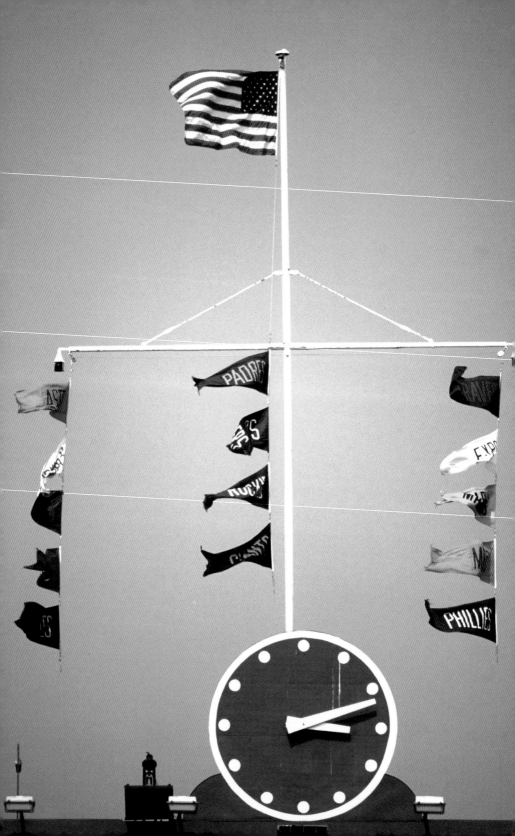

fans who just hated the whole idea. Finally, on April 8, 1988, the scene was set; lights would, for the first time, brighten a Cubs game at Wrigley Field. A huge crowd was expected. Broadcaster Harry Caray (see box, page 102) would, for the first time, lead the crowd in a nighttime version of *Take Me Out to the Ballgame* during the seventh-inning stretch. In the long and often sad history of the Cubs, it was to be a momentous occasion.

Of course, this being the Cubs, it rained. The game was called after three innings.

The lights went on the next night ("Cubs win! Cubs win!" bellowed Caray in his trademark post-victory cry, as they knocked off the Mets 6-4). Today about 25 percent of the team's home games are played at night. Though it's a big change from the "old days," there is something uniquely beautiful about sitting high atop the center-field bleachers, beneath the huge, hand-operated scoreboard, as the fans stand on Waveland Avenue behind the left-field bleachers awaiting high-flying home run balls. For a night game, you sit up there and the skyline of Chicago pops up like metal corn to your left, the setting sun turning buildings a misty orange. To your right, the west, the fading sun spreads its glow on a prairie as flat as an outfield stretching out to the Rockies. You can see forever to one side or you can admire the beauty of man's creation to the other, but your view always dips instead toward the field, the emerald green grass, the rusty red brick, the perky ivy, and the ghosts that roam the outfield in the twilight.

....

Left: The clock above the Wrigley Field center-field scoreboard (shown here in 1996) is just one of the many clever adornments installed in 1937. The NL team flags are changed daily to reflect the standings. **Following pages:** Wrigley Field was the last Major League ballpark to install lights for night games. This picture shows a night game in 1997.

....

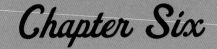

Chapter Six

YANKEE STADIUM

T he places where Major League Baseball was played, until 1923, were "parks," or "fields," or "grounds." In 1923, a new colossus arose, and it was no mere ballyard, no mere meadow; it was a *stadium*, muscular, huge, dominant, the first in the game's history to take that name. It was Yankee Stadium, and it would become the site of more important and famous moments in the history of the sport than just about anywhere.

Its genesis came from the team's success, most notably caused by Babe Ruth. The slugging outfielder had joined the Yankees for the 1920 season and proceeded to change the way the game was played. Cracking 54 homers in 1920, topping the previous record (also held by Ruth) by 25 homers, and then whacking 59 more in 1921, Ruth helped the Yankees outdraw the Giants at the Polo Grounds, where both teams played. In fact, the Yankees set a Major League attendance record in 1920, becoming the first team to draw one million fans. Not surprisingly, the Giants were less than pleased to be second-class citizens in their own backyard, so they ordered the Yankees out. In *Diamonds*, author Michael Gershman notes that Giants manager John McGraw said at the time, "[The Yankees] won't be able to find another location in Manhattan. They'll have to move to the Bronx . . . the fans will

Following pages: The colossal Yankee Stadium, shown here at its opening on April 18, 1923, signaled a new era in ballpark construction.

forget about them and they'll be through." Falser words were never spoken.

Yankees owners Jacob Ruppert and Tillinghast Huston did, in fact, explore other sites in Manhattan and even in Queens. They ended up, as McGraw predicted, in the Bronx, on 10 acres across the river from the Polo Grounds. There they put into action a plan for something that would match their newfound power, on the field and at the box office. They put up a stadium for the ages. Its triple decks soared above the field, and seats there and in the outfield bleachers could hold an astounding 58,000 fans. Around the upper rim of the inside of the stadium was the architectural detail that helped define the place, a series of bridge-like scallop shapes forming a famous frieze. The huge triple decks (the first in the Majors), were originally planned to ring the park, but at first extended only to the foul poles in each corner. Above the bleachers in right field, fans on the elevated train track and station could peer down into the bowl of the stadium and see much of the field. The team offices were moved from midtown Manhattan to locations inside the stadium itself, in an area above home plate.

"It was no mere ballyard, no mere meadow; it was a *stadium*, muscular, huge, dominant, the first in the game's history to take that name."

Built in less than a year, Yankee Stadium opened on April 18, 1923, with more than 72,000 people squeezed in during these years of more lenient fire laws. They all saw what they came to see: Ruth smacking a home run into the right-field seats. (Knowing Ruth's predilections, Ruppert & Co. had put the right-field corner only 295 feet from home plate. No Polo Grounds,

---

Right: One of the defining architectural details of Yankee Stadium is the frieze along the roof of the upper deck, shown here during the 1961 World Series. **Following Page:** Lou Gehrig (number 4) greets the Babe after Ruth crosses the plate during the 1932 World Series.

YANKEE STADIUM

Ballpark Basics

Location: Bronx, New York, 161st St. and River Ave.

Date opened: April 18, 1923

Approximate cost: $2.5 million

Tenants: New York Yankees, 1923–present

Outfield distances: Left field: 318 feet; Left-center field: 399 feet; Center field: 408 feet; Right-center field: 385 feet; Right field: 314 feet

Largest crowd: 85,265, on September 9, 1928

Capacity (2003): 56,000

Home team W-L record: New York Yankees at home (1923–1973, 1976–present): 3,873-2,285 (through 2003)

First home run: Babe Ruth, New York Yankees (April 18, 1923)

Last home run: not applicable

Player with most home runs: Mickey Mantle, New York Yankees (266)

Number of no-hit games pitched (and most recent): 11 (six Houston Astros pitchers combined for a no-hitter on July 11, 2003)

Other events/sports: Many heavyweight boxing matches have been held here, including Max Schmeling's upset of Joe Louis in 1936, Louis' victory in the rematch in 1938, and Ingemar Johansson's upset of Floyd Patterson in 1959 . . . Pro football home of various incarnations of the New York Yankees, as well as the New York Giants (1956–1973)...Site of the famous NFL Championship Game in 1958 between the Baltimore Colts and the Giants (the first sudden-death overtime game in league history) . . . Soccer great Pele played in the stadium while a member of the New York Cosmos in the 1970s.

Unusual ground rules: The original monuments in left-center field were in play . . . In the 1930s, any ball that hit the foul pole was in play (it was not a home run).

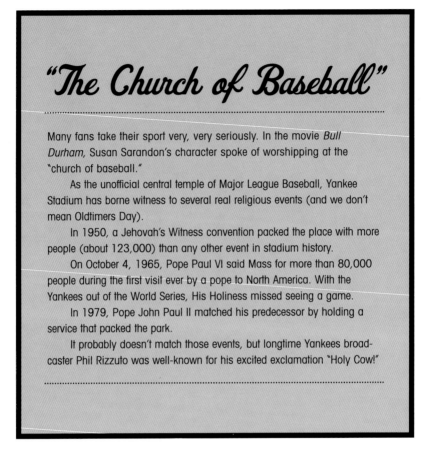

"The Church of Baseball"

Many fans take their sport very, very seriously. In the movie *Bull Durham*, Susan Sarandon's character spoke of worshipping at the "church of baseball."

As the unofficial central temple of Major League Baseball, Yankee Stadium has borne witness to several real religious events (and we don't mean Oldtimers Day).

In 1950, a Jehovah's Witness convention packed the place with more people (about 123,000) than any other event in stadium history.

On October 4, 1965, Pope Paul VI said Mass for more than 80,000 people during the first visit ever by a pope to North America. With the Yankees out of the World Series, His Holiness missed seeing a game.

In 1979, Pope John Paul II matched his predecessor by holding a service that packed the park.

It probably doesn't match those events, but longtime Yankees broadcaster Phil Rizzuto was well-known for his excited exclamation "Holy Cow!"

to be sure, but pretty close nonetheless.) Legendary sportswriter Fred Lieb wrote that the new baseball palace was "The House That Ruth Built," and that nickname has stuck.

The Stadium hosted its first of 34 World Series that season, and the Yankees twisted the knife into their former roommates, defeating the Giants in six games.

Additional changes in the ensuing years included extending the triple decking into left field, adding several scoreboards, and changing the outfield bleachers from wood to concrete.

Over the next several decades, those seats were witness to a series of momentous events. Here are just a few:

• September 30, 1927: Babe Ruth became the first player in history to reach 60 homers in a season when he hit a pitch from Washington's Tom Zachary into the right-field seats. It would be the single-season mark for 34 years.

• July 4, 1939: Stricken with amyotrophic lateral sclerosis (ALS), the disease that would soon bear his name, Lou Gehrig made a memorable speech at a day in his honor. The Hall of Fame first baseman, the "Iron Horse" who played 2,130 consecutive games, one of the game's greatest all-time hitters, Gehrig that day elevated himself above his athletic exploits. Knowing he would never play again and was facing an unknown enemy (it would take his life less than two years later), Gehrig nonetheless called himself "the luckiest man on the face of the earth." Yankee Stadium itself continues to play a part in this heroic moment, as Gehrig's oft-heard words were recorded echoing around the great stadium.

Above: Yankees star "Joltin'" Joe DiMaggio, the "Yankee Clipper" (in the 1940s).

• July 2, 1941: Joe DiMaggio hit safely in his 45th consecutive game, breaking the old mark set by "Wee" Willie Keeler in 1897. DiMaggio's streak would eventually reach an unthinkable 56 straight games; it was brought to an end not in the Bronx, but in Cleveland on July 17.

• June 13, 1948: The Stadium once again had a starring role in a memorable goodbye. One of the most famous photos in the game's history shows an aging and frail Babe Ruth, his bold number 3 on his pinstriped back, against a backdrop of a packed stadium. The scalloped frieze frames the portrait as Ruth looks up toward the cheering crowd. His number was retired, and while his farewell words were not as poignant as Gehrig's, the sentiment was. The man who "built the House" died less than two months later. His body lay in state at the stadium and more than 100,000 people filed past to pay their respects.

• October 8, 1956: Don Larsen pitched the only perfect game in World Series history. Not a single Brooklyn runner reached base in Larsen's 97-pitch gem. Considered a journeyman pitcher, Larsen nonetheless put together an unprecedented and unmatched string of zeroes in the 2-0 victory, which came in Game 5 of a World Series the Yankees won in seven games. It's worth noting that of the 16 perfect games pitched in Major League Baseball history (through 2003), three have taken place at Yankee Stadium, more than at any other park. David Wells in 1998 and David Cone in 1999 joined Larsen in this trio of perfection.

• October 1, 1961: In the 163rd and final game of the season (the Yankees had one tie that year), Roger Maris of the Yankees whacked a pitch from Boston's Tracy Stallard into the seats for his 61st home run of the season, breaking Ruth's record. The blast

Right: Babe Ruth says farewell to the crowd at Yankee Stadium, June 13, 1948.
Following pages: The view from the upper deck at Yankee Stadium (1996).

The 1958 NFL Championship Game

The "Greatest Game Ever Played" in Yankee Stadium was *not*, according to some historians, a Major League Baseball game; it was a football game—the 1958 NFL Championship Game between the Baltimore Colts and the hometown New York Giants. The "Jints" (Giants) played their home games in Yankee Stadium from 1956 to 1973. It's worth noting that among other parks in this book, Tiger Stadium was home to the Detroit Lions while Fenway Park occasionally played host to the Boston (later New England) Patriots. Wrigley Field was the original home of the Chicago Bears; in fact, that team's ursine name was inspired by its parkmate's.

In 1958 the Giants and Colts faced off in a game that remains today among the seminal moments in American sports. Until this game, Major League Baseball had ruled the sports world, with the NFL playing second, or in some places third, fiddle. But a new and growing medium, television, was just coming into vogue and football proved to be the perfect TV sport. With a field that "fit" the TV screen, action that created numerous commercial breaks, and a time limit that created finite broadcasts, football would become the king of the airwaves. Its coronation was this game.

The action was fierce and furious, with the two teams taking and retaking the lead from each other. With less than two minutes to go in regulation, Baltimore's Johnny Unitas, perhaps the finest quarterback in NFL history, drove his team to a tying field goal as regulation time ended. The game thus became the first major sports championship that would be decided in overtime.

Unitas put together another masterful drive in OT, connecting on key passes while calling all his own plays. He handed off to Alan "The Horse" Ameche from the one-yard line and as Ameche fell into the end zone, the game ended with Baltimore a 23-16 winner, and a new era in football began. And it did so on the infield dirt of Yankee Stadium.

Left: Yankee Stadium, shown here circa 1997, has hosted a variety of events in its long and storied career.

came amid controversy, however, as Ruth accomplished his feat during a 154-game season; at first, Maris' mark was recorded with an asterisk noting the disparity in games. In later years, cooler heads prevailed, and Maris' 61 was the record Mark McGwire aimed at in 1998 when he became the first player to top that total.

In 1974, the Yankees moved out of Yankee Stadium while a renovation was undertaken by the city of New York, which had become the stadium's owner. View-obscuring columns were removed, the entire upper deck was rebuilt, the playing field was lowered, the wooden seats were replaced with plastic, and the famous copper frieze was mostly removed. That motif was kept in many places, however—notably across the huge outfield scoreboard, which now featured one of the first video replay screens in the Major Leagues. The cost of all this work was borne by the City of New York, in an effort to keep the Yankees from leaving town, which the new owners, led by George Steinbrenner, had threatened. Newspaper estimates ranged as high as $160 million for all the work—much higher than the initial plans called for—and some taxpayer groups complained bitterly.

> "Maris' mark was recorded with an asterisk noting the disparity in games. In later years, cooler heads prevailed . . . ."

As they had when the stadium first opened, the Yankees not only inaugurated the renovated park in 1976 with a victory (11-4 over Minnesota), but they also made it to the World Series. Though they lost to Cincinnati, they did win it all in 1977 and 1978.

In 1983, another famous incident occurred at Yankee Stadium: the "pine tar" home run hit by Kansas City Royals star

Left: Outfielder Roger Maris, shown here circa 1962, beat the Babe's single-season home run record with 61 in 1961. **Following pages:** Outside the impressive home-plate gate of Yankee Stadium in 2000.

Magical Moments

September 30, 1927
Babe Ruth hits his then-record 60th home run of the season.

October 8, 1927
The Yankees complete a four-game sweep of the Pirates
for their second of a record 26 World Series championships.

July 4, 1939
Lou Gehrig Day at Yankee Stadium, honoring the heroic ballplayer.

July 2, 1941
On his way to 56 straight, Joe DiMaggio hits safely
in his 45th consecutive game, breaking the old mark
set by "Wee" Willie Keeler in 1897.

June 13, 1948
Babe Ruth says goodbye.

October 8, 1956
New York's Don Larsen pitches the only perfect
game in World Series history.

October 1, 1961
Roger Maris sets a new single-season record with his 61st home run.

October 18, 1977
Reggie Jackson's three homers help the Yankees
clinch a World Series victory over the Dodgers.

October 26, 1996
The Yankees win their first World Series in 18 years, beating the
Atlanta Braves four games to two.

July 18, 1999
Following David Wells' perfect game in 1998, David Cone
makes it three perfect games in Yankee Stadium
history by blanking the Expos 5-0.

George Brett. On July 24, Brett hit a home run with two outs in the ninth to take the lead over the Yankees. He touched home plate, and then New York manager Billy Martin protested to umpires that the pine tar, a sticky substance used by hitters for a better grip, extended too far up Brett's bat, breaking a rule. The umps agreed and ruled Brett out, causing Brett, the Hall of Fame third baseman, to break from the dugout like a lion after an impala. After a lengthy argument and a protest by the Royals, the game was called.

Later, AL president Larry McPhail said the umps were wrong, and that the game would be replayed from that point. The Royals returned to Yankee Stadium on August 18, where the game ended quietly with a Kansas City victory.

Less controversial and much more celebratory have been recent events at Yankee Stadium, including the 1996 World Series victory for the Yankees, their first in 18 years. After this World Series, third baseman Wade Boggs joined a cop atop a police horse to ride around the field in triumph. The Yankees and their fans also enjoyed world titles in 1998, 1999, and 2000. That last was against the crosstown New York Mets in a "Subway Series" reminiscent of the great contests the Bronx

> "As they had when the stadium first opened, the Yankees not only inaugurated the renovated park in 1976 with a victory (11-4 over Minnesota), but they also made it to the World Series."

Bombers held with the Brooklyn Dodgers and New York Giants in the 1950s. In 2003, Aaron Boone won the ALCS for the Yankees with a dramatic 11th-inning, walk-off homer that defeated the rival Boston Red Sox.

For victory, for championships, for grandeur, nothing matches Yankee Stadium. Its massive size keeps it from earning the charming jewel box status enjoyed by other still-extant historic parks, but Yankees fans will take pennants over ivy and monsters any day.

The Plaques

Large monuments to Lou Gehrig, longtime manager Miller Huggins, and Babe Ruth were at one time on the field of play in center field. Huggins' came first, followed by Gehrig's and Ruth's after their deaths. Following the 1976 renovation, a "Monument Park" was created behind the left-field fence, and the monuments were joined there by plaques honoring baseball greats as well as important Yankee Stadium visitors. Before most games, fans can walk through the small area near the bullpens and view these famous pieces of bronze. Here is a complete list of people honored in Monument Park.

Lou Gehrig	Thurman Munson
Miller Huggins	Don Mattingly
Babe Ruth	Whitey Ford
Ed Barrow	Roger Maris
Jacob Ruppert	Ron Guidry
Joe DiMaggio	Mel Allen (broadcaster)
Mickey Mantle	Bob Sheppard (stadium announcer)
Casey Stengel	Phil Rizzuto
Lefty Gomez	Billy Martin
Allie Reynolds	Reggie Jackson
Yogi Berra	Pope Paul VI
Bill Dickey	Pope John Paul II
Elston Howard	
Joe McCarthy	

Right: Hall of Famer Lou Gehrig, pictured here in 1939, was one of many stars to wear Yankees stripes. **Following pages:** Monument Park, once part of the field of play, is now a walled-off shrine to the great figures who have walked the aisles of Yankee Stadium (shown here in 1994).

INDEX

Photo Credits

About the Author

James Buckley Jr. has written more than thirty books on baseball and other sports for adults and young readers, including *Perfect: The Story of Baseball's 16 Perfect Games; Baseball: A Celebration; The Visual Dictionary of Baseball;* and *Sports Immortals*. After working as an editor and writer for Sports Illustrated and NFL Publishing and contributing to numerous national magazines, Buckley founded the Shoreline Publishing Group in 1999; the company is a book producer specializing in sports books. A former youth baseball coach, he is on the board of directors of the four-time California state champion Santa Barbara Foresters semipro team.